THE LAST WORD

THE LAST WORD

Reflections on a Lifetime
of Preaching

JOHN STOTT

Authentic

MILTON KEYNES • COLORADO SPRINGS • HYDERABAD

14 13 12 11 10 09 08   7 6 5 4 3 2 1
First published 2008 by Authentic Media
9 Holdom Avenue, Bletchley, Milton Keynes, Bucks, MK1 1QR, UK
1820 Jet Stream Drive, Colorado Springs, CO 80921, USA
OM Authentic Media, Medchal Road, Jeedimetla Village, Secunderabad
500 055, A.P., India
www.authenticmedia.co.uk

Authentic Media is a division of IBS-STL U.K., limited by guarantee, with its
Registered Office at Kingstown Broadway, Carlisle, Cumbria CA3 0HA. Registered
in England & Wales No. 1216232. Registered charity 270162

British Library Cataloguing in Publication Data
A catalogue record for this book is available from the
British Library
ISBN-13: 978-1-85078-794-5

Cover Design by David Smart
Print Management by Adare
Printed in the UK by CPI William Clowes Beccles NR34 7TL

CONTENTS

FOREWORD

It truly would be an irony if, in introducing an author whose concern is that we should become like Christ, we were to distract from that focus by talking too much about the messenger. But the Council of Keswick Ministries felt it appropriate to express our gratitude to God and to Dr John Stott for his contribution to Keswick and, indeed, to the work of God around the world. I am glad to do so by way of a brief introduction to this book, and the intention is to glorify the Lord Jesus himself, whom John Stott so faithfully serves.

I suppose that most of us would associate John Stott with a particular church – All Souls, Langham Place, in the heart of London – where, in 1950, he was appointed rector at the age of 29. Although for nearly sixty years he has travelled to every corner of the globe, the All Souls family has been the church to which he has ministered and the church which has supported him in his national and global ministry.

Under God, John Stott has had a profound influence on the church in the UK, whether through his writing or preaching, or through particular initiatives such as his engagement with the National Evangelical Anglican Congress, or chairing the Church of England Council. But he has exercised an influence well beyond the Anglican Communion, not least in his strategic leadership as President of organisations such as Scripture Union, the Evangelical Alliance, and the Universities and Colleges Christian Fellowship. His contribution in the UK has also been marked by his service as a Chaplain to the Queen, a position he has held for over thirty years. Then we are thankful for his concern to encourage the church to think Christianly about every area of the modern world, which led him to establish the London Institute for Contemporary Christianity in 1982. This has been just one influential outworking of his conviction that the whole of life must be lived under the Lordship of Jesus Christ.

His influence has not only been felt in the UK. By God's grace, John Stott has also had a major impact on the church around the world. This was expressed early on through his university missions, held on campuses in many different countries, and also through his work as Vice-President of the International Fellowship of Evangelical Students. He has had a considerable impact on the cause of global mission, not only through his writings but also through his engagement in organisations such as the Lausanne Movement for World Evangelisation. But in particular he is known as a tireless advocate and friend of the church in the majority world – in the continents of Africa, Asia and Latin America – the 'global south' where the church has been growing so rapidly under such extraordinary pressure. John Stott is known by believers throughout those continents and countries as 'uncle John', and is held in much affection by church leaders and church members in country after country. He has founded several programmes particularly to serve that part of the global church family, which have been amalgamated under the name of Langham Partnership International. Following John Stott's original motivation some 35 years ago, under the leadership of Dr Chris Wright it seeks to help the church grow to maturity by equipping preachers and teachers. It does so through the distribution and creation of good books, by supporting theological education for gifted young men and women in the majority world, and also by encouraging national preaching movements designed to train and support pastors and lay preachers all around the world.

Indeed, John Stott's concern for issues of poverty in that part of the world has also been expressed by his presidency of Tear Fund. He also holds a strong doctrine of creation, and is concerned about our care for the natural world. He is an avid bird watcher and photographer, having spotted around 2,700 species, and published a book entitled *The Birds Our Teachers* – introducing the theme of 'ornitheology', as he would say.

This leads us to Dr Stott's writing – which has had the most far-reaching influence. His fifty books have been shaped by a clear commitment to the gospel and strong evangelical convictions, and they are always characterised by three things: a faithfulness to the Bible as the word of God, a relevance to the contemporary world in which we live, and a remarkable clarity of expression. By way of example, he has edited the IVP flagship

Bible Speaks Today series (New Testament), which combines the best in evangelical scholarship with pertinent contemporary application. *The Cross of Christ*, recently reissued in a twentieth anniversary edition, still represents a leading evangelical contribution on the subject, and his *Issues Facing Christians Today* has been updated over the years to keep it at the cutting edge of active, practical Christianity. These are some of the memorable titles that Dr Stott has produced, which have strengthened the Church globally in both its understanding and its mission. His work has been translated into many languages and has profoundly impacted Christians around the world. So it is no wonder that this global reach has been recognised by his being named in *Time* magazine's 'One hundred most influential people' in 2005 (sharing a page with Bill Gates), and by being named in the Queen's New Year Honours list as a CBE in 2006.

But all of this aside, countless people around the world can testify to the godly influence and the deep encouragement brought to bear on their Christian lives and on their Christian communities through uncle John's personal example. His biographer,

Timothy Dudley Smith, has expressed it in this lovely paragraph

> To those who know and meet him, respect and affection go hand in hand. The world figure is lost in personal friendship, disarming interest, unfeigned humility and a dash of mischievous humour and charm. By contrast, he thinks of himself, as all Christians should but few of us achieve, as simply a beloved child of a heavenly Father, an unworthy servant of His friend and Master Jesus Christ, a sinner saved by grace, for the glory and praise of God.

It was therefore a special honour that Keswick Ministries was able to welcome John Stott to address the Convention in the summer of 2007, and we are delighted that his timely and moving address is now being made available to a wider audience. May this small book encourage every reader to devote their lives wholeheartedly to the joyful pursuit of Christ-likeness.

Jonathan Lamb
On behalf of the Council of Keswick Ministries
July 2007

John Stott Stott was born in London in 1921, and educated at Rugby School and Trinity College, Cambridge. At Trinity, he earned a double first in French and Theology, and was elected a senior scholar. He trained for the pastorate at Ridley Hall, Cambridge, and was awarded a Lambeth doctorate in divinity in 1983. He has honorary doctorates from America, Britain and Canada. Following his ordination in 1945, John Stott became Assistant Curate at All Souls and then, unusually, went on to become Rector in 1950. He became Rector Emeritus in 1975.

THE MODEL – BECOMING LIKE CHRIST

WHAT IS GOD'S PURPOSE?

I remember very vividly, some years ago, that the question which perplexed me as a younger Christian (and some of my friends as well) was this: what is God's purpose for his people? Granted that we have been converted, granted that we have been saved and received new life in Jesus Christ, what comes next? Of course, we knew the famous statement of the Westminster Shorter Catechism: that man's chief end is to glorify God and to enjoy him forever: we knew that, and we believed it. We also toyed with some briefer statements, like one of only five words – love God, love your neighbour. But somehow neither of these, nor some others that we could mention, seemed wholly satisfactory. So I want to share with you where my mind has come to rest as I approach the end of my pilgrimage on earth and it is – God wants his people to become like Christ. Christlikeness is the will of God for the people of God.

So if that is true, I am proposing the following: first to lay down the biblical basis for the call to

Christlikeness: secondly, to give some New Testament examples of this; thirdly, to draw some practical conclusions. And it all relates to becoming like Christ.

THE BIBLICAL BASIS FOR THE CALL TO CHRISTLIKENESS

This basis is not a single text: the basis is more substantial than can be encapsulated in a single text. The basis consists rather of three texts which we would do well to hold together in our Christian thinking and living: Romans 8:29, 2 Corinthians 3:18 and 1 John 3:2. Let's look at these three briefly.

Romans 8:29 reads that God has predestined his people to be conformed to the image of his Son: that is, to become like Jesus. We all know that when Adam fell he lost much – though not all – of the divine image in which he had been created. But God has restored it in Christ. Conformity to the image of God means to become like Jesus: Christlikeness is the eternal predestining purpose of God.

My second text is 2 Corinthians 3:18: 'And we all, with unveiled face, beholding the glory of the Lord, are being changed into his likeness, from one degree of glory to another; for this comes from the Lord who is the Spirit.' So it is by the indwelling

Spirit himself that we are being changed from glory to glory – it is a magnificent vision. In this second stage of becoming like Christ, you will notice that the perspective has changed from the past to the present, from God's eternal predestination to his present transformation of us by the Holy Spirit. It has changed from God's eternal purpose to make us like Christ, to his historical work by his Holy Spirit to transform us into the image of Jesus.

That brings me to my third text: 1 John 3:2. 'Beloved, we are God's children now and it does not yet appear what we shall be but we know that when he appears, we will be like him, for we shall see him as he is.' We don't know in any detail what we shall be in the last day, but we do know that we will be like Christ. There is really no need for us to know any more than this. We are content with the glorious truth that we will be with Christ, like Christ, for ever.

Here are three perspectives – past, present and future. All of them are pointing in the same direction: there is God's eternal purpose, we have been predestined; there is God's historical purpose, we are being changed, transformed by the Holy Spirit;

and there is God's final or eschatalogical purpose, we will be like him, for we shall see him as he is. All three, the eternal, the historical and the eschatalogical, combine towards the same end of Christlikeness. This, I suggest, is the purpose of God for the people of God. That is the biblical basis for becoming like Christ: it is the purpose of God for the people of God.

WE ARE TO BE LIKE CHRIST . . .

In his Incarnation

I want to move on to illustrate this truth with a number of New Testament examples. First, I think it is important for us to make a general statement, as the apostle John does in 1 John 2:6: 'he who says he abides in Christ ought to walk in the same way as he walked.' In other words, if we claim to be a Christian, we must be Christlike. Here is the first New Testament example: we are to be like Christ in his Incarnation.

Some of you may immediately recoil in horror from such an idea. Surely, you will say to me, the Incarnation was an altogether unique event and cannot possibly be imitated in any way? My answer to that question is yes and no. Yes, it was unique, in the sense that the Son of God took our humanity to himself in Jesus of Nazareth, once and for all and forever, never to be repeated. That is true. But there is another sense in which the Incarnation was not unique: the amazing grace of

God in the Incarnation of Christ is to be followed by all of us. The Incarnation, in that sense, was not unique but universal. We are all called to follow the example of his great humility in coming down from heaven to earth. So Paul could write in Philippians 2:5–8

> Have this mind among yourselves, which was in Christ, who, though he was in the form of God, did not count equality with God some thing to be grasped for his own selfish enjoyment, but emptied himself, taking the form of a servant, being born in the likeness of men. And being found in human form he humbled himself and became obedient unto death, even death on a cross.

We are to be like Christ in his Incarnation, in the amazing self-humbling which lies behind the Incarnation.

In his service

We move on now from his Incarnation to his life of service; from his birth to his life, from the beginning to the end. Let me invite you to come with me to the upper room where Jesus spent his last evening with his disciples, recorded in John's gospel chapter 13

> He took off his outer garments, he tied a towel round him, he poured water into a basin and washed his disciples' feet. When he had finished, he resumed his place and said, 'If then I, your Lord and Teacher, have washed your feet, you also ought to wash one another's feet, for I have given you an example' – notice the word – 'that you should do as I have done to you.

Some Christians take Jesus' command literally and have a foot-washing ceremony in their Lord's Supper once a month or on Maundy Thursday – and they may be right to do it. But I think most of us transpose Jesus' command culturally: that is just as Jesus performed what in his culture was the work of a slave, so we in our cultures must regard no task too menial or degrading to undertake for each other.

In his love

I think particularly now of Ephesians 5:2 – 'walk in love as Christ loved us and gave himself up as a fragrant offering and sacrifice to God.' Notice that the text is in two parts. The first part is 'walk in love', an injunction that all our behaviour should be characterised by love, but the second part of the verse says that he gave himself for us, which is not a continuous thing but an aorist, a past tense, a clear reference to the cross. Paul is urging us to be like Christ in his death, to love with self-giving Calvary love. Notice what is developing: Paul is urging us to be like the Christ of the Incarnation, to be like the Christ of the foot washing and to be like the Christ of the cross. These three events of the life of Christ indicate clearly what Christlikeness means in practice.

In his patient endurance

In this next example we consider not the teaching of Paul but of Peter. Every chapter of the first letter of Peter contains an allusion to our suffering like Christ, for the background to the letter is the beginnings of persecution. In chapter 2 of 1 Peter in particular, Peter urges Christian slaves, if punished unjustly, to bear it and not to repay evil for evil. For, Peter goes on, you and we have been called to this because Christ also suffered, leaving us an example – there is that word again – so that we may follow in his steps. This call to Christlikeness in suffering unjustly may well become increasingly relevant as persecution increases in many cultures in the world today.

IN HIS MISSION

Having looked at the teaching of Paul and Peter, we come now to the teaching of Jesus recorded by John. In John 20:21, in prayer, Jesus said 'As you, Father, have sent me into the world, so I send them into the world' – that is us. And in his commissioning in John 17, he says 'As the Father sent me into the world, so I send you.' These words are immensely significant. This is not just the Johannine version of the Great Commission but is also an instruction that their mission in the world was to resemble Christ's mission. In what respect? The key words in these texts are 'sent into the world'. As Christ had entered our world, so we are to enter other people's worlds. It was eloquently explained by Archbishop Michael Ramsey some years ago: 'We state and commend the faith only in so far as we go out and put ourselves with loving sympathy inside the doubts of the doubters, the questions of the questioners and the loneliness of those who have lost the way.'

This entering into other people's worlds is exactly what we mean by incarnational evangelism. All authentic mission is incarnational mission. We are to be like Christ in his mission. These are the five main ways in which we are to be Christlike: in his Incarnation, in his service, in his love, in his endurance and in his mission.

THE PRACTICAL CONSEQUENCES OF CHRISTLIKENESS

Christlikeness and the mystery of suffering

Suffering is a huge subject in itself and there are many ways in which Christians try to understand it. One way stands out: that suffering is part of God's process of making us like Christ. Whether we suffer from a disappointment, a frustration or some other painful tragedy, we need to try to see this in the light of Romans 8:28–29. According to Romans 8:28, God is always working for the good of his people, and according to Romans 8:29, this good purpose is to make us like Christ.

Christlikeness and the challenge of evangelism

Why is it, you must have asked, as I have, that in many situations our evangelistic efforts are often fraught with failure? Several reasons may be given and I do not want to over-simplify but one main reason is that we don't look like the Christ we are proclaiming. John Poulton, who has written about this in a perceptive little book entitled *Today's Sort of Evangelism*, wrote this

> The most effective preaching comes from those who embody the things they are saying. They are their message. Christians need to look like what they are talking about. It is people who communicate primarily, not words or ideas. Authenticity gets across. Deep down inside people, what communicates now is basically personal authenticity.[1]

That is Christlikeness. Let me give you another example. There was a Hindu professor in India who once identified one of his students as a Christian and said to him: 'If you Christians lived like Jesus Christ, India would be at your feet tomorrow.' I think India would be at their feet today if we Christians lived like Christ. From the Islamic world, the Reverend Iskandar Jadeed, a

---

[1] Poulton, J., *Today's Sort of Evangelism* (Cambridge: Lutterworth Press, 1972).

former Arab Muslim, has said 'If all Christians were Christians – that is, Christlike – there would be no more Islam today.'

Christlikeness and the indwelling of the Spirit

I have spoken much tonight about Christ-likeness but is it attainable? In our own strength it is clearly not attainable but God has given us his Holy Spirit to dwell within us, to change us from within. William Temple, Archbishop in the 1940s, used to illustrate this point from Shakespeare

It is no good giving me a play like Hamlet or King Lear and telling me to write a play like that. Shakespeare could do it – I can't. And it is no good showing me a life like the life of Jesus and telling me to live a life like that. Jesus could do it – I can't. But if the genius of Shakespeare could come and live in me, then I could write plays like this. And if the Spirit could come into me, then I could live a life like His.

So I conclude, as a brief summary of what we have tried to say to one another: God's purpose is to make us like Christ. God's way to make us like Christ is to fill us with his Spirit. In other words, it is a Trinitarian conclusion, concerning the Father, the Son and the Holy Spirit.

AFTERWORD

I just want to add a word of personal testimony ... I was brought up in a home and a church where I learned in my early years to really love the Bible. And in my early teens, I could quote John 3:16 and Romans 3:23, and I could probably even teach some lessons from those verses. But if in my mid-teens you had asked me, for example, 'What is the argument of the Book of Romans?', I wouldn't have been able to answer you.

Then one day in my mid-teens, I picked up John Stott's commentary on the Book of Galatians, and that book completely transformed the way I read, studied and understood Scripture. I could see that books needed to be studied as books; that verses needed to be studied within their context. Simple and obvious but, for me, transformational.

And as I look back over the last forty years, I see how books from Dr Stott and sermons that I have listened to have had a huge impact upon my life. *The Christian Mission to the Modern World* has shaped my understanding of mission, and significantly impacted the way mission is understood within Operation Mobilisation. That great Lausanne Congress that Jonathan referred to, and the Lausanne Covenant which came from that Congress, which John Stott was so influential in drafting – its impact on Christian mission is, I believe, almost incalcuable. Time and time again, when we in mission are struggling with missiological and strategic issues, we go back to that Statement. *Issues Facing Christians Today* helped me think through, and come to a biblical position, on so many ethical issues I was grappling with. The Bible Speaks Today commentary on the Sermon on the Mount has a particular place in my life. It's challenged me, time and again, on the way I live my daily life and the way I handle the relationships of my life.

When I first read *The Cross of Christ*, I can only say my response was worship, as I read such a succinct statement of what was accomplished at the cross. I have gone back to that book again and again to clarify issues which surround that event, which is at the very heart of our faith. And I could go on and speak of many other books and sermons which have had a deep impact on my life.

I have had no formal theological education. There's a sense in which Dr Stott has been my New Testament lecturer, with his New Testament commentaries and his editing of the BST New Testament series. He has been my ethics lecturer, with *Issues Facing Christians Today*. He's been my Missions lecturer, with *The Christian Mission in the Modern World*, and he has been my lecturer on Christian doctrine with such books as *The Cross of Christ*. I am having a wonderful Keswick week, as my Old Testament lecturer is here too – Alec Motyer.

Recently I met a group of international mission leaders, thirty of us, many from the global south. We were discussing in devotions one morning who were the most significant mentors in our lives. And I responded that, for me, John Stott is the most significant mentor in my life. Not through very much personal contact but through books and through tapes. There is no doubt that he has shaped my thinking probably more than anyone else. When I sat down, one after another of these mission leaders, about thirty, stood up and gave a very similar testimony. So let's thank God today, together, for a man being so greatly used in the service of the Kingdom.

Peter Maiden
Chair of the Council of Keswick Ministries
July 2007

JOHN STOTT INTERVIEW

**Dr John Stott was interviewed by
Brian Draper of LICC**

BD: Twenty-five years ago, you were instrumental in setting up the London Institute of Contemporary Christianity, and we have not yet done ourselves out of a job. I wonder if you can tell us, why did you set up the Institute in the first place?

JS: Clearly, there is no one reason. Several things came together, and I would like to mention them, if I may. I was talking one day to a couple of students: one was at Oxford and the other one at Edinburgh University. I knew that they had been brought up in a conservative Christian home but I also knew that now they were repudiating the faith of their parents. So I said to them 'Tell me about it. What has happened to you? Is it that you no longer believe that Christianity is true?' 'No,' they said, 'that is not our problem, and if you could persuade us that Christianity is true, we are not at all sure that we would accept it.' 'Oh,' I said, with mounting surprise. They said, 'Christianity is a primitive Palestinian religion. What has it got to say to us, who live in the exciting modern world? We have men on the moon in the seventies' – they were speaking some years ago – 'and we shall have men on Mars in the eighties' (they were a bit optimistic) – 'so what has your primitive Palestinian religion got to say? It's irrelevant.'

I am not going to tell you how I replied, because I did very badly, but God used that interview to challenge me – not to make Christianity relevant, as if it isn't, but to demonstrate its relevance. Demonstrating the relevance of the gospel was one of the major factors in founding the Institute. Maybe I could go on and mention another reason, because they do go together. We had an assistant minister at that time at All Souls church. He was a New Zealander, a brash colonial, and his name was Ted Schroeder. He worked among students in the Polytechnic and his great concern was to relate the gospel to the modern world. It was then that he challenged me about my preaching. He said that my preaching was maybe accurate in its exposition, but it was irrelevant. I didn't relate it to the modern world. That challenged me too. There were two challenges which the Institute was designed to meet: how to think Christianly and how to relate the word to the world.

BD: Can you remember how the idea of the Institute was initially received?

JS: I think it was greeted warmly by those who knew about Regent College, Vancouver. I myself had been teaching in Summer Schools at Regent College, and they had pioneered the way in developing an Institute to help people to think Christianly. It is very important, I think, to remind ourselves that the London Institute is a lay Institute. It is not a place for training pastors or for training missionaries. It is a lay Institute, designed deliberately for professional people, for business people, to help them to think about their work Christianly and to go back into their job and into their world with a stronger perspective on what they are doing as Christians.

BD: How would you assess the impact of the Institute over the last twenty-five years?

JS: What surprised us at the beginning was that the majority of students who came and hungrily ate up what we had to tell them were not Brits. Some were from Europe but mainly they were from the majority world. In my travels in those days, I was constantly meeting bright young professional people – lawyers, doctors, sociologists and so on – who were longing to find a context within which they could think about their jobs and about their citizenship. And then they would come particularly to the 'Christian in the Modern World' school, and go back with a new determination to be a Christian in every branch of their lives. We spent a lot of time in those early days trying to shape exactly what it was we were trying to do, and we came up with four things which have remained part of that particular course. The first is interpreting the Bible. From the very beginning, we had this great concern to develop principles of biblical interpretation which were sound, solid and could be relied on. This was my own responsibility in the early lectures. Secondly, understanding the modern world:

these students came from the modern world and we needed to help them understand it more profoundly. Thirdly, living as disciples. And fourthly, reaching out in mission, so that faith, conduct and mission blended with one another. People have seen that in order to be an out-and-out follower of Jesus, you don't have to become a pastor, you don't have to become a missionary – it's a great mistake to imagine that you must. So we laid our emphasis on the Lordship of Jesus. We knew, of course, that 'Jesus is Lord' is the fundamental Christian creed. It's the shortest and simplest of all Christian creeds, and not only does it tell us who Jesus was and is – the Lord – but it also tells us what is required of us, namely radical discipleship. I love that word 'radical' – going down to the roots – and we believe that Jesus demands from his disciples such radical discipleship.

BD: John, the world has changed a lot in the last twenty-five years or so. Are there principles that we can actually come back to, time and again, which help us to become more effective whole life followers of Jesus, in whatever culture we find ourselves?

JS: I've been very struck in my own study of the Holy Scriptures to see that there are many themes throughout its pages, but there is one theme which we have tended to neglect, and that is the call to be different from the world around us. It's interesting to me that in the four great sections of the Bible, the same call comes out: in the law, in the prophets, in the gospels and in the epistles. These are the four great sections, and in each one there is the same call. Think for example of Leviticus and the law: God says through Moses to the children of Israel, 'You shall not do as they do in the land of Egypt in which you lived and you shall not do as they do in the land of Canaan to which I am bringing you. You shall not follow their statutes, you shall follow my decrees and my laws.' It's a remarkable statement. It's often found in the prophets, where Israel was accused of following the nations around them. Then we can jump to the Sermon on the Mount. I love that verse in Matthew 6, 'Do not be like them', Jesus said. Just five mono-syllables. Then, of course, in the epistles we have Romans 12: 'Do not be conformed to the world around you.' That is absolutely fundamental to all our thinking, that we are called to follow Jesus and his standards, and to reject the way of the world around us.

BD: You once said that if LICC ceased to exist, then someone would have to reinvent it immediately. I wonder why that is, and is our task here a continual one?

JS: Let me introduce the phrase 'double listening', which has always been a significant phrase for me. It means, of course, that we are called to listen both to the word of God and to the modern world, in order to relate the one to the other. So we listen first to the word of God, mainly of course in Scripture. Evangelical people like ourselves tend to claim that we know our Bibles, but there's a challenge that needs to be brought to the church again, that maybe we don't know them as well as we think we do, and there is a need for us to penetrate deeply into Scripture in order to understand and obey what God has said in his word. But then we also need to listen to the voices of the modern world. Now having said that, we don't listen to the voices of the modern world with the same degree of respect with which we listen to the voice of God.

We listen to the voice of God in order to understand it and obey it: we don't necessarily obey the voices of the modern world. We have to sift them, to discern what is from God and what isn't. But it is in this double listening – listening to the word of God and listening to the voices of the modern world – only then is it possible for us to relate the one to the other. We must understand both before we can relate the two together.

BD: So how have you, in your life, tried to do this double listening?

JS: I would want to take the two together, the voices in this double listening. I would want to say a bit more about the word of God. There is a need for us to penetrate deeply into what God has said. So much of our Bible reading is simplistic. I hope that doesn't sound over-critical, but I think we need to penetrate the Bible more profoundly. Granted, most of us do read the Scriptures regularly. I'm very grateful to the late Dr Martyn Lloyd Jones who, fifty years ago, introduced me to the lectionary that was produced by Robert Murray McCheyne of Dundee in 1842, if I remember rightly. He wanted his whole congregation to read the whole Bible through every year – the New Testament twice, the Old Testament once. In the lectionary we have to read four chapters a day, which is a considerable task. The interesting thing is that on January 1st we do not begin with Genesis 1 – 4, and January 2nd with Genesis 5 – 8. Instead, we start with the four great beginnings of Scripture, that is Genesis 1, Ezra 1, Matthew 1 and Acts 1. These are the four great beginnings of Scripture, the four great births: the birth of the Universe, the birth of the nation of Israel, the birth of Jesus and the birth of the Christian community. There are four beginnings, and it is fascinating to read through, seeing how they relate to one another. So the great themes emerge, then disappear and reappear, and so on. So I'm a great believer in encouraging people to do that kind of thorough Bible study. But I would like to go on and say that, for most of us, it is probably more important that we should study the modern world. For me, this meant starting a reading group. Somewhere around 30 to 40 years ago I invited a dozen young professional people to join me in a reading group in London. We had an architect, two doctors, a teacher and so on, and we met, sometimes once a month, sometimes every two months. We began by sitting in a circle and each was given half a minute or so in which to identify what he or she believed was the most important matter raised by the book that we had all supposedly read. Over the years we read dozens and dozens of books, and I can only say that these young professional people dragged me screaming into the modern world. I would strongly recommend it to others today. So it is both reading the Bible, and studying the modern world – and putting them in relation to each other.

BD: The authority of the Bible is clearly an important issue here, isn't it?

JS: Defending the authority of the Bible has certainly been something that has been of great importance to me all through my life, because I have seen - as we all must see - that this is a vital part of our Christian pilgrimage. To me, it's bound up with the authority of Christ. The authority of Christ and the authority of Scripture belong or fall together. Jesus stood in the middle between the two Testaments. He looked back to the Old Testament and affirmed its authority: he looked forward to the New Testament, deliberately calling his apostles and equipping them to be the bearers of his word. So to look back to the Old Testament and to look on to the New Testament (and the authority of the apostles) still seems to me a satisfactory basis on which to base one's confidence.

The relation of Scripture to culture is again another vital question. There is a danger that those whom we would call liberal theologians tend to say, 'Oh well, this teaching is only a cultural thing, it doesn't necessarily have authority over us.' Of course, there are cultural things which are temporary or of transient authority, and it is important for us to learn which is which. But one thing I would want to say is that what creation has established, no culture is able to destroy. So we need to discern what is fundamental, what is creational. Old questions like 'Should women wear hats or veils in church?' – that kind of thing – are very clearly a cultural matter. So is the braiding of the hair, for example. We don't need to follow those things in any degree of detail, because they are cultural and are different in different cultures. So a

Ugandan girl, for example, would be horrified to be told she can't braid her hair. All Ugandan women do, and rightly so – it's their culture.

BD: Within these questions of confidence in Scripture, defending truth, the authority of Scripture, have you ever experienced doubt and do you allow for doubt within your faith?

JS: Yes, of course. I think anyone who denies it is less than human. The question of doubt is part of our humanity, it is part of the kind of person that God has made us. Having said that, I would want to illustrate from the story of Thomas. We tend to have sympathy for him, but Jesus didn't. Jesus said to him, 'Blessed are those who have not seen but believe', and his position was that Thomas ought to have believed the other apostles, because he knew that they were reliable men and they claimed they had seen the Lord. He had no reason to doubt their claim. Faith rests on testimony – it rests on reliable testimony – and the question to ask ourselves is, 'Is the testimony of the apostles in the New Testament reliable?' Having said that, I'd want to come back and say that there is a difference between doubting on the one hand and questioning on the other. Questioning is a very healthy attitude. We know that from childhood: children are asking questions, and rightly so, because that is the way in which they grow up. So don't let's be afraid of asking questions, but let's remember when we're doubting that we can go back to the beginnings, to the claims of Jesus, to the evidence for the resurrection, to two thousand years of Christian tradition, and all of the things on which we base our faith. I think that kind of doubt should be transient: questioning should be permanent.

BD: And as you've grown older, have you continued to ask those questions?

JS: I have, partly because I've been challenged to do so. You may know that I was involved in the writing of a book, some ten to fifteen years ago, in which I was debating with a well-known liberal historian and theologian. It was published under the title *Essentials*. We agreed that he would lay down his questions but that I would be given the opportunity to respond to each of them, one by one. I found that he was entirely lacking in authority. The phrase he continually used was that 'the climate of educated opinion was . . .' this, that or the other, and I had to challenge him and say 'But we have a stronger authority than the climate of educated opinion.' I had to face his questions. You asked me a personal question, as to whether I have ever doubted or questioned. The answer is yes, because when you are up against a liberal theologian of his ability, you're pretty shaken, but I think I can honestly say that, slowly but surely, I was able to think my way through the serious questions he was asking.

BD: You were cited by *Time* magazine, famously, in 2005, as being one of its one hundred most influential people in the world. You don't always like to talk about it but why do you think that was, and how do you actually try to use your influence?

JS: Let's begin by saying that when I first read that in *Time* magazine – and I had no idea they were going to publish it, of course – but when I read it, I literally burst out laughing, because it is so utterly absurd. There must be hundreds of thousands of people whose influence is greater than mine. I may have had a little influence, under God, in some spheres, but I'm certainly not one of the one hundred most influential people in the world. I forget which leading American politician asked 'Why is flattery like cigarette smoking?' The answer is 'It does you no harm so long as you don't inhale.' I believe, as an ordinary Christian, I've had to struggle to allow flattery to be like water off a duck's back – mainly because I know it isn't true. Humility is not another word for hypocrisy, pretending to be other than you are. Humility is another word for honesty, understanding who you are and how you have become what you are.

BD: How would you most like to be remembered?

JS: I think probably I would say in the ways in which you and I have been discussing today. When I talk about the authority of Scripture and the application of the word to the world, this is something of very profound significance to me in my personal life. How would I like to be remembered? I think as an ordinary Christian who has struggled in his desire to understand, to expound and to relate and apply the word of God. I think that is how I would like to be remembered.

BD: When do you feel most alive?

JS: Spiritually speaking, I think I would have to say 'in public worship'. I think I know what it is, in public worship, to be transported above and beyond myself, into a world of ultimate reality, with angels and archangels and all the company of heaven. And I think there is almost nothing that convinces me more of the reality of God than public worship. With a congregation, one is just lifted into heaven. So that's one. I think another, and quite different one, would be in terms of human friendships. I'm grateful to have many friends, and very grateful to have the opportunity to enjoy their friendship and to do things with them.

BD: Birdwatching?

JS: You know I'm a rather fanatical birdwatcher, or I used to be. My eyesight is deteriorating and I can't really see now, ornithologically speaking, as I used to be able to. People have asked me how I began to be a birdwatcher and the answer is really through my father. My father was a physician, a cardiologist to be precise, and during the summer holidays he would take me out for walks in the country and tell me to shut my mouth and open my eyes and ears – which is a splendid illustration of observation. I began by being hooked on butterflies. I had two sisters and one of them was always my rival. We got into an argument together, and she threw a cushion at me which landed in the middle of my butterfly box. If I've ever seen red in my life, I saw it then. I chased her round and round the table in the nursery, and I reckon I would have killed her, if I'd caught her, but I didn't catch her. My butterflies were ruined. My father did his best to mend them with Seccotine or other kinds of glue, but I was utterly disconsolate for a week. But now – it's an interesting example of divine providence – now, I'm very thankful that I did change from butterflies to birds. People think I'm peculiar enough to go round the world with a pair of binoculars, but supposing I had gone round the world with a butterfly net – I doubt if I would have survived! What is so wonderful about birds or butterflies, or anything in nature, is that it is so marvellous, early in the morning, to go out before the world is awake, to enjoy all the sights and the sounds and the smells of nature, to get away from people. I think I've experienced what you're talking about, in those three ways, and probably in others as well.

BD: You stayed as Rector of All Souls, Langham Place, when I'm sure there must have been all sorts of possibilities opening up for you – the world of academia, ascending the hierarchy of the Church of England, even marriage. If you had your time again, would you make that same decision and did you really sense that this was a strong calling, a vocation?

JS: Yes, I think it was. As I think you have said without realising it, there are probably three major decisions I have made in my life, three renunciations, if you like. One was against an academic career when I was at Cambridge. My professors were urging me to stay in Cambridge, to get a fellowship at one of the colleges and to pursue an academic career. It was very attractive but I was convinced that God had not called me to that but rather to a pastorate. Then, of course, there was marriage, as you rightly say. I was expecting to marry. I went about with a weather eye, and in my twenties and early thirties was looking for a possible bride. All I can say – and I did have two girlfriends, not simultaneously but one after t'other! – all I can say is that, when the time came to decide whether to go forward in the relationship or not, I lacked the assurance that I should go forward. That is the only way I can really explain it. And the third is the ecclesiastical hierarchy, whether to become a Bishop or an Archbishop . . . and once again, I believed that God had called me to the pastorate.

BD: Are we less willing these days, do you think, to count the cost of discipleship?

JS: I've been very challenged by the three-fold refrain in Luke's gospel, chapter 14, where Jesus stops in the road, turns round to face his disciples and says to them, 'If any man comes after me and does not hate his family, renounce riches, money and turn away even from himself, he cannot be my disciple'. So there is the cost of discipleship, and I believe that actually applies to all of us, those three things. Not to hate, of course, since what Jesus meant was that we must love him more than any human relationship. But yes, I think we need to be more honest in laying out for people what is involved in the cost of discipleship.

BD: Are you optimistic about the world and the church's role within it?

JS: Yes and no, which is the answer that one desires to give to all of your questions! Yes, because faith and optimism belong together: we can't be believers and not be optimists, in the sense that we believe that God is on the throne and that he knows what he is doing, and we can trust him.

BD: I think that from everything you're saying, it's imperative that the work of LICC continues.

JS: Each new generation needs to be challenged afresh. It may not be the same people who are exposed to the same challenges, but each genera-tion is followed by the next and the next, and they do need to be challenged. It's an indispensable part of our Christian discipleship – not to separate the secular from the sacred, but to allow Jesus to become Lord in every sphere of our lives. You can't be a Christian without facing these things, and so we have to face them in every generation.

BD: Thank you for speaking to us.

THE PRIVILEGES OF THE JUSTIFIED

1. Peace with God – Romans 5

Chapters 5 – 8 of the epistle to the Romans are without doubt among the greatest and most glorious of the whole New Testament. They portray in great fullness what I have called 'The Privileges of the Justified.' The earlier chapters of the Epistle are devoted to the need and the way of justification (how all men are sinners under the just judgement of God; and how only through the redemption that is in Christ Jesus can they be justified, by grace alone through faith alone). And now, having enforced the need, and unfolded the way, of justification, Paul describes its fruits, its results (especially a life of sonship and obedience here, and of glory hereafter).

This is important because too many of us think and behave as if the Gospel were only good news of justification, and not good news also of holiness and of heaven; as if (having come to God through Christ) we had arrived; as if we had come to a dead end, and there were no further road to travel. But this is not so! This section of the Epistle begins (5:1), 'Therefore, being justified by faith (having been brought into acceptance with God through trust in Christ) . . .' and the apostle goes on at once to indicate the consequences.

These chapters, then, depict the great privileges of justified believers, the rich inheritance (both now and in eternity) which is ours if we are Christ's. I have called these privileges, first, *Peace with God* (chapter 5); second, *Union with Christ* (chapter 6); third, *Freedom from the Law* (chapter 7); and fourth, *Life in the Spirit* (chapter 8).

1. Peace with God (chapter 5)

Romans 5 is actually in two clearly distinct paragraphs. The first eleven verses summarise the fruits of our justification, while verses 12–21 portray the mediator of our justification. He is Jesus

Christ, the second Adam, the one man through whose one deed justification has been won for us.

(a) The Fruits of our Justification (vv. 1–11)

In verses 1 and 2 the fruits of justification are summed up in three sentences:

(i) v1: We have peace with God through our Lord Jesus Christ.
(ii) v2a: We have obtained access (through the same Christ by the same faith) into this grace in which we stand.
(iii) v2b: We rejoice in hope of God's glory.

Here are the major fruits of our justification – peace with God (which we have), grace (in which we stand), and glory (for which we hope).

On closer examination, these appear to relate to the three tenses or phases of our salvation.

'Peace with God' speaks of the *immediate* effect of justification. We were enemies (v10), but the old enmity has been put away by God's forgiveness, and we are now at peace with him through our Lord Jesus Christ. That is the immediate effect of justification. 'This grace in which we stand' speaks of the *continuing* effect of justification. It is a state of grace, to which we have obtained access, and in which we continue to stand. 'We have been allowed to enter the sphere of God's grace' (NEB); now we are standing in it. 'The glory of God,' for which we hope, speaks of the *ultimate* effect of justification. 'The glory of God' means heaven, since in heaven God himself will be fully revealed ('glory' is God revealed); we shall see his glory and share in it. 'Hope' is our sure and certain confidence or expectation of it. Indeed, so sure is this hope (this 'happy certainty' – J.B. Phillips) that we can rejoice in it now already. We give thanks for it in the General Thanksgiving in the words 'for the means of grace and for the hope of glory'.

These phrases constitute a beautifully balanced summary of the Christian life in relation to God (nothing is yet said about our duty to our neighbours) – 'peace,' 'grace' and 'glory'. These are the fruits of justification. In the word 'peace' we look back to the enmity which is now over. In the word 'grace' we look up to our reconciled Father in whose favour we now continue to stand. In the the word 'glory' we look on to our final destiny, seeing and reflecting the glory of God, which is the object of our hope or expectation.

Not that, after justification, the narrow way is carpeted only with moss and primroses; No! Brambles grow on it, too – and brambles with sharp thorns. Verse 3, 'More than that' (RSV) 'we rejoice in our sufferings'. These sufferings are not, strictly speaking, sickness or pain, sorrow or bereavement, but tribulation, the pressures of a godless and hostile world.

Such suffering is always the pathway to glory. The risen Lord said so, namely that according to the Old Testament, 'the Christ should suffer and so enter into his glory.' The apostle Peter, echoing these words, also said so several times in his first epistle. The apostle repeats that in 8:17, 'provided we suffer with him in order that we may also be glorified with him.'

But please note what is to be the relation between our present sufferings and our future glory. It is not just that the one is the way to the other. Still less is it that we grin and bear the one in anticipation of the other. No, it is that we *rejoice* in both. If we rejoice in hope of the glory of God (v2), we rejoice in our sufferings also (v3). The verb is strong: it indicates that we 'exult' in them (NEB). Present suffering and future glory are both objects of a Christian's exultation.

How is this? How can we possibly rejoice in sufferings, and find joy in what causes us pain? Verses 3–5 explain the paradox. It is not the sufferings themselves which we rejoice in, so much as their beneficial results. We are not masochists, who enjoy being hurt. We are not even Stoics, who grit their teeth and endure. We are Christians, who see in our sufferings the working out of a gracious divine purpose. We rejoice, because of what suffering 'produces' (RSV). What does it produce? What are the outworkings of tribulation?

Three stages in the process may be discerned:

Stage 1: 'Suffering produces endurance' (RSV). The very endurance which we need in suffering is produced by it, much as 'antibodies' are produced in the human body by infection. We could not learn endurance without suffering, because without suffering there would be nothing to endure.

Stage 2: 'Endurance produces character' (RSV). 'Character' (AV, 'experience') is the quality of something which, or someone who, has stood the test. It is the quality David's armour lacked, because he had not 'proved' it. Can we not usually recognise the ripe character of those who have gone through suffering and come out triumphant? 'Suffering produces endurance, and endurance character.'

Stage 3: 'Character produces hope.' That is, confidence of future glory. The character, which has a maturity born of past endurance of suffering, brings a hope of future glory. What Paul means is surely this, that our developing, ripening Christian character is evidence that God is at work upon and within us. And he who is maturing us through suffering will surely and safely bring us to glory. The apostle is back, you see, to the indissoluble link between sufferings and glory. The reason why, if we rejoice in hope of the glory of God, we rejoice in our sufferings also, is that our sufferings produce hope (through producing endurance and character). If the hope of glory is produced by sufferings, then we rejoice in the sufferings as well as the glory; we rejoice not only in the end, but in the means which bring us there.

But how can we know that this hope has substance to it, and is not wistful thinking? Paul asserts: 'Hope does not (that is, will not) disappoint us' (RSV) or 'such a hope is no mockery' (NEB). It is a true hope. But how can we be so sure? Paul's answer to this unspoken question is in the rest of verse 5: 'because God's love has been poured out (perfect tense) in our hearts through the Holy Spirit who was given to us' (literally). The solid foundation on which our hope of glory rests is the love of God. It is because God has set his love upon us that we know he is going to bring us safely to glory. We believe we are going to persevere to the end, and we have good grounds for this confidence. It is partly because of the character God is forming in us through suffering ('suffering–endurance–character–hope' is the order); and if he is thus sanctifying us now, he will surely glorify us then. But it is chiefly because of the love that will not let us go.

This is the argument: We have a Christian hope, that we are going to see and share in the glory of God. We believe this Christian hope is a sure hope. It is 'no mockery.' It will never disappoint us. We know this because we know that God loves us and will never let us down, never let us go.

But how do we know that God loves us? The answer is, because we have an inner experience of it: 'God's love has flooded our inmost heart through the Holy Spirit He has given us' (v5, NEB). The Holy Spirit has been given to every believer, and one of the works of the Spirit is to pour out God's love into our hearts, to flood our hearts with it, that is, to make us vividly and inwardly aware that God loves us. Or, as Paul expresses the same truth in chapter 8, to witness with our spirit that we are God's children and that he is our Father who loves us. The change of tense in the verbs of verse 5 is noteworthy. The Holy Spirit was given to us (*aorist*), a past event; God's love has been poured out into our hearts (*perfect*), a past event with abiding results. The Holy Spirit was given to us when we believed. At the same time he flooded our hearts with God's love. He still does. The flood remains; it continues. The once given Spirit caused a permanent flood of divine love in our hearts.

Let me sum up what we have learned so far. The fruits of justification are peace with God (the enmity over); grace as a state in which we stand; and a hope (a joyful confident expectation) of the glory of God. This is a hope produced by the character that God is working in us through the endurance of suffering, but a hope that is confirmed by the assurance of God's love which the

Holy Spirit has given us. In other words, justification (which is itself a momentary act, a judicial decision of our righteous God who pronounces us righteous in Christ) yet leads to a permanent relationship to God summed up in the words 'grace' now, and 'glory' at the end – a state of grace now in which we stand, and glory at the end for which we hope, a hope grounded upon God's love which through the Spirit has flooded our hearts.

We turn now to verses 6–11, in which the fruits of justification are further revealed. In verses 1–5, Paul has joined peace and hope, justification and glorification, making *our* sufferings the link. In verses 6–11 he does it again, but this time makes *Christ's* sufferings and death the link.

Let us see what he tells us here about the death of Jesus. He reminds us that Christ died for the utterly undeserving. This is the emphasis of verses 6–11. We may begin by seeing the unflattering terms with which we are described. Four terms are used. We are called 'helpless' (v6), because we are unable to save ourselves. We are 'ungodly' (v6), because we are in revolt against the authority of God. We are 'sinners' (v8), because we have missed the mark of righteousness, however hard we may have tried to aim at it. And we are 'enemies' (v10), because of the hostility which exists between us and God. What a fearful, devastating description of man in sin! We are failures, rebels, enemies and helpless to save ouselves. Yet it is for *such* people that Jesus Christ died!

We would hardly die for a *righteous* man (one who is coldly upright in his conduct), although perhaps for a *good* man (warm and attractive in his goodness) some people would even dare to die (v7). But God shows *his* love (the word is emphatic, his own love, his unique love) in giving Christ to die for *sinners*. Not for the coldly upright, not even for the attractively good, but for sinners – unattractive, unworthy, undeserving.

This is the setting for his argument, which follows in verses 9–11. It is an *a fortiori*, a 'much more' argument, an argument from the lesser to the greater, which reaches up to a new truth by standing on the shoulders of an old one. Paul contrasts the two main stages of salvation, justification and glorification, and shows how the first is the guarantee of the second. Let us try to grasp the details of his contrast between these two salvations, present and future.

First, he contrasts what they are. Verse 9, 'Since we are now justified by his blood, much more shall we be saved through him from the wrath of God.' Here the contrast is plain, between our present justification and our future salvation from the wrath of God on the day of judgment. If we are already saved from God's *condemnation* (because we are justified), much more shall we be saved from his *wrath*.

Secondly he contrasts how they are achieved. Verse 10, 'For if while we were enemies we were reconciled to God by the death of his Son, much more, now that we are reconciled, shall we be saved by his *life*.' Here the emphatic contrast is between the *death* of God's Son and his *life*. That is, the risen life of Christ in heaven will complete what the death of Christ began on earth. The best commentary on this truth is probably 8:34, 'Who can condemn? It is Christ – Christ who died, and more than that, was raised from the dead – who is at God's right hand and indeed pleads our cause,' completing by his life what he accomplished by his death.

Thirdly, he contrasts the people who receive them. This again is in verse 10. It was while we were *enemies* that we were *reconciled* to God by the death of his Son. Much more shall we be saved by his life now that we are *reconciled* to him. If God reconciled his *enemies* he will surely save his *friends*!

There is, in other words, a strong argument or presumption that we are going to inherit a full and final salvation; that we shall not be allowed to fall by the way, but shall be preserved unto the end, and glorified. This argument is not a sentimental optimism; it is grounded upon irresistible logic. If when we were enemies God reconciled us through giving his Son to die for us, how much more, now we are his friends, will he finally save us from wrath through his Son's life? If God performed the more costly service (involving his Son's death) for his enemies, he will surely do the easier and less costly service now that his erstwhile enemies have become his friends.

More than that (v11); the Christian life is not just looking back to justification and on to glorification. The Christian is not preoccupied always with the past and the future. He has a present Christian life to live. So 'we rejoice in God through Jesus Christ.' We rejoice in hope. We rejoice in our sufferings also. But above all, we rejoice in God himself. And we do it through Jesus Christ. It is through Jesus Christ that we have peace with God (v1). It is through Jesus Christ we have obtained access into the grace in which we stand (v2). It is through the blood of Christ that we have been reconciled, and through the life of Christ that we are going to be saved (v9). It is through Jesus Christ that we have received (*aorist*) the reconciliation. It is a present possession which we enjoy. So we rejoice in God through the Christ who has achieved these priceless blessings for us.

Or is time now for us to look back over the first paragraph of chapter 5 (vv1–11).

In both parts of it (vv1–5, and 6–11) the apostle's thought moves from justification to glorification, from what God has already done for us, to what he is still going to do for us in the consummation. Thus (vv1,2) having been justified by faith, we rejoice in hope of the glory of God; and in verses 9 and 10, being justified by his blood, we shall be saved from wrath. So both parts argue from our present salvation to our final salvation, from our justification to our glorification.

Further, both parts speak of the love of God, and build our assurance of final salvation upon it. See verses 5 and 8. If we Christians dare to say that we are going to heaven when we die, and that we are sure we shall be finally saved, it is not because we are self-righteous or self-confident. It is because we believe in the steadfast love of God; the love that will not let us go.

Moreover, both parts provide some ground for believing that God loves us. These grounds are two – objective and subjective. The objective ground for believing that God loves us is *historical*; it concerns the death of his Son (v8). The subjective ground for believing that God loves us is *experimental*; it concerns the gift of his Spirit (v5). God proves his love at the cross (notice in verse 8 that though a past event, the tense is present); and according to verse 5, God has poured his love into our hearts. So we know that God loves us. We know it rationally as we contemplate the cross (God gave his best for the worst). We know it intuitively as the Holy Spirit floods our hearts with a sense of it.

In each case the apostle links to this knowledge our assurance of final salvation. 'Hope does not disappoint us' (v5). That is, we know that our expectation of final salvation will be fulfilled. It is well grounded. It will not deceive or disappoint us. How do we know? 'Because the love of God has been shed abroad in our hearts.' Again, in verses 8–10, how do we know that we shall be saved from wrath? Answer, because God proves his love for us by having given his Son to die for us while we were sinners.

Is there a Christian here who is full of doubts about his eternal salvation; who knows that he has been justified but has no assurance that all will be well at the end? Let me emphasise again that final glorification is the fruit of justification – 'whom he justified, them he also glorified' (8:30). Trust in the God who loves you! Look at the cross, and accept it as God's own proof of his love for you! Then ask him to flood your heart with his love by his Spirit! Then away with gloomy doubts and fears! Let them be swallowed up in the steadfast love of God.

We turn now from (a) the fruits of our justification (vv1–11) to (b) *the mediator of our justification* (vv12–21). In the first paragraph Paul has traced our reconciliation and final salvation to the death of God's Son. His exposition immediately prompts the question: but how can one person's sacrifice have brought such blessings to so many? It is not (in Sir Winston Churchill's famous expression) that so many owe so much to *so few*; it is that so many owe so much to *one person*! How can that be? The apostle answers this anticipated question by drawing an analogy between Adam and Jesus Christ. (And incidentally, the strongest argument for the historicity of Adam is not scientific, but theological. The Christian believes in the historicity of Adam, not even just because of the Old Testament story, but because New Testament theology requires him to do so). Both Adam and Jesus Christ demonstrate the principle that *many* can be affected (for good or ill) by *one* person's deed.

Verses 12–14 concentrate on Adam: 'As sin came into the world through one man and death through sin, and so death spread to all men because all men sinned.' This verse sums up in three stages the history of man before Christ. (i) Sin entered into the world through one man. (ii) Death entered into the world through sin, because death is the penalty for sin. (iii) Death spread to all men, because all men sinned (this is explained later). These are the three stages: sin – death – universal death. That is, the present situation of universal death is due to the original transgression of one man.

In verses 13–14, this progression (from one man sinning to all men dying) is further explained. Death is visited upon all men today, not because all men have sinned *like* Adam, but because all men sinned *in* Adam. This is plain, Paul argues, because of what happened during the time between Adam and Moses, between the Fall and the giving of the Law. During that period people certainly sinned, but their sins were not reckoned against them because sin is not reckoned when there is no law. Yet they still died. Indeed (v14) 'death reigned from Adam to Moses, even over those whose sins were not like the transgression of Adam.' So, Paul argues, logically, the reason they died is not that they deliberately transgressed like Adam, and died for their transgression, but that they and the whole of humanity were involved and included in Adam, the head of the human race. It is because we sinned in Adam, that we die today.

At the end of verse 14, however, the apostle calls Adam 'a type of the coming one,' and with verse 15 the analogy between Adam and Christ begins; an enthralling analogy containing both *similarity* and *dissimilarity*. What is the same is the pattern:

that many are affected by one man's deed. What is different is the motive, and the nature, and the effect of the one man's deed (Adam's and Christ's), that is, the *motive* for the deed, or why he did it; the *nature* of the deed, or what he did; and the *effect* of the deed, or what happened as a result.

(a) *The motive* (v15a). This is seen in the contrast of verse 15, between 'the offence' and 'the free gift' ('the free gift is not like the trespass,' RSV), for 'the offence' was a deed of sin, a deviation from the path, while 'the free gift' was a deed of grace. Adam's deed was one of *self assertion*, going his own way; Christ's deed was one of *self sacrifice*, of free, unmerited favour (stressed in the following words).

(b) *The effect* of the deed (vv. 15b–17). Reference to the opposite effects of the work of Adam and Christ is already anticipated at the end of verse 15, where the sin of one man brought to many the grim penalty of *death*, whereas the grace of God and of one man, Jesus Christ, abounded to many in bestowing a free *gift*, which according to 6:23 is *eternal life*. So death and life are contrasted; and the next two verses (16, 17) elaborate the opposite effects of the deeds of Adam and of Christ. 'The judgment following one trespass brought condemnation, but the free gift following many trespasses brings justification' (v16b, RSV). 'If, because of one man's trespass death reigned through that one man, much more will those who receive the abundance of grace and the free gift of righteousness reign in life through the one man Jesus Christ' (v17, RSV).

These, then, are the contrasting effects of the deeds of Adam and of Christ. The sin of Adam brought condemnation; the work of Christ brings justification. The reign of death is due to Adam's sin; a reign of life is made possible through Christ's work. The contrast could not be more complete; it is in fact absolute, between condemnation and justification, and between death and life.

It is noteworthy, however, exactly how the apostle contrasts life and death. It is not just that the reign of death is superseded by a reign of life, for (v17) it is not life which reigns but *we* who are said to reign in life. Formerly death was our king and we were its subjects, slaves, under its totalitarian tyranny. We do not now exchange that kingdom for another, so that we are in another sense slaves, or subjects. No. Delivered from the rule of death, we begin to rule over it and over all the enemies of God. We cease to be subjects, and ourselves become kings, sharing the kingship of Christ.

(c) *The nature* of the two deeds (verses 18, 19). We have seen that Adam's deed and Christ's deed were different in their motive (what prompted them) and in their effect (what resulted from them). Now the apostle contrasts the two deeds themselves, in their nature. The parallel drawn is similar to what has gone before, but the emphasis in verses 18 and 19 is now on what Adam and Christ did. According to verse 18, what led to condemnation for all was one man's *offence*, and what led to justification and life for all (in Christ) was one man's *righteousness*. Adam's 'offence' was a failure to keep the law; Christ's 'righteousness' (RSV, 'act of righteousness') was a fulfilment of the law.

According to verse 19, it is by one man's *disobedience* that many were made sinners, and by one man's *obedience* that many will be made righteous.

Adam disobeyed the will of God and so fell from righteousness; Christ obeyed the will of God and so fulfilled all righteousness (cf. Matt. 3:15; Phil. 2:8). Looking back over the paragraph, we see a striking and significant contrast between Adam and Christ. As to the *motive* for their deeds: Adam asserted himself; Christ sacrificed himself. As to the *nature* of their deeds: Adam disobeyed the law; Christ obeyed it. As to the *effect* of their deeds: Adam's deed of sin brought condemnation and death; Christ's deed of righteousness brought justification and life.

So, then, whether we are condemned or justified, alive or dead, depends on which humanity we belong to – the old humanity initiated by Adam, or the new humanity initiated by Christ. And this in its turn depends on our relation to Adam and to Christ. All men are in Adam, since we in Adam by *birth*. But not all men are in Christ, since we are in Christ by *faith*. In Adam by birth we are condemned and die; but if we are in Christ by faith, we are justified and live.

This brings us back to the privileges of the justified with which we began, because these are only ours in and through Jesus Christ. Verse 1, 'we have peace with God *through our Lord Jesus Christ*.' Verse 2, '*through Him* we have obtained access to this grace in which we stand, and we rejoice in our hope of sharing the glory of God.' 'Peace,' 'grace' and 'glory' (the privileges of the justified) are given not to those who are in Adam, but only to those who are in Christ.

This chapter is taken from the title John Stott at Keswick *(978-1-85078-808-9) which is a compilation of the all talks given by John Stott at the Keswick Convention.*

OF HUMILITY AND WHOLE-LIFE DISCIPLESHIP

John Stott and The London Institute for Contemporary Christianity

'Jesus Christ is Lord,' If the London Institute for Contemporary Christianity had a text, this, so said John Stott at our Silver Jubilee Celebration in 2007, would be it. Philippians 2:11: Jesus Christ is Lord of all, Lord of all creation, Lord of every aspect of our lives and every aspect of our humanity – intellectual, emotional, relational, sexual, ecological, political . . . In 1982, however, the reality was that the vast majority of Christians had no such comprehensive vision. Sadly, this remains the case. Back then, the charge facing Christianity was not so much that it was perceived to be untrue but, as John put it, to be 'trivial'. The challenge was to demonstrate that the Bible did indeed speak to the issues, concerns and yearnings of late 20th century people, not only to satisfy the mind and soothe the heart but to shape a life worth living and transform society.

And so, with others, John founded the London Institute, not so much to help people develop responses to 'issues facing Christians today', though that was certainly part of it, but more importantly to work out how to help Christians live out every aspect of their life as disciples of Jesus Christ. Indeed, the heart of LICC's work for its first twenty years was a ten week residential discipleship course called 'The Christian in the Modern World'. It attracted Christians from all over the world – Africa, Asia, North and South America and continental Europe. It attracted doctors and lawyers as well as pastors and missionaries, teachers and business people as well as student workers and administrators. Here then representatives of the global church wrestled together to grow in interpreting and applying the Bible, in engaging with culture, in living as whole-life disciples and in living out the missional life – wherever God called them.

Steve Beck, a 'graduate' of the course in 1984, and subsequently LICC's Chairman for nine years, put it this way, 'The London Institute ruined me for life.' It wasn't, however, the period of his chairmanship that left such an indelible mark but his experience of that ten week course. It 'ruined' his life because afterwards there was no going back to a comfortable, private, individual Christian faith. Christ's Lordship applied to everything – public and private, work and leisure, individual and community. Indeed, the fruit of those courses has been extraordinary – in business, in healthcare, in initiatives among the poor, in the development of leadership and training institutes like LICC all round the world, in the ministries of pastors and leaders in countless organisations.

In hindsight, other people's decisions often seem inevitable to us, but the more I think about the foundation of the London Institute for Contemporary Christianity the more remarkable it seems. Not many people start organisations at the age of forty, fewer still at the age of fifty, and even fewer at the age of sixty. Indeed, although John Stott was aided and abetted in the development of the idea by a number of talented Christian leaders and supported by many friends, in the end it was he who shouldered the yoke. Why?

After all, John already had a fruitful global writing and speaking ministry, why take on the messy business of running an Institute? Why spend time getting involved with people from all over the world for ten week courses? Why not just write another book? Take another trip? I wonder if it had something to do with the way Jesus made his disciples – in close relationship, over meals, with plenty of time and opportunity for questions and answers.

Beyond that, I am continually struck by John's extraordinary humility. Imagine for a moment that you are widely regarded as one of the finest preachers in the world and then some young curate has the temerity to challenge your ability to apply the word of God in a relevant way to people's daily lives. How might you respond? It is, after all, one thing to change something that is not appreciated by others, it's quite another to change something that you do brilliantly in order to try to do it better. Similarly, it is not at all obvious that you would change the thrust of your internationally affirmed ministry on the basis of a conversation with two sceptical, non-believing students. But that is what John did. He listened with discernment and responded with determination.

Still, if discernment and determination might characterise the foundation of LICC, 'warmth' and 'friendship' are the words that come to mind when we at LICC think of John's ministry there. As David Limebear, a good friend of mine, once said of John, 'He had a genius for friendship.' And also for spotting talent and potential. He made people feel that they were significant to him, that their question was important, their life in Christ vital, their talents and calling precious. Of course, that was because he believed all those things and expressed that belief in so many different ways. Certainly through diligent prayer, but also by never allowing students to get away with woolly thinking or sloppy expression. In any interaction, John sacrificed neither truth nor love.

One former student remembers working late on a project in LICC's seminar room. John walked in and asked him if he would like a cup of tea. The student demurred. Surely the Reverend Dr John R.W. Stott had other things to do. But the tea was served to the young disciple, just as fish were served on a Galilee shore to other young disciples two thousand years before.

There never was any doubt who John was following.

Mark Greene
Executive Director, The London Institute for
Contemporary Christianity
www.licc.org.uk

LANGHAM PARTNERSHIP INTERNATIONAL

Growing a new generation of preachers and teachers

For many years, John Stott travelled in the majority world of Africa, Asia and Latin America. In his contact with Christian leaders in these countries, he would frequently discuss the challenges and opportunities that confronted the church. If you were to ask such leaders what was their number one problem, they would invariably reply 'growth without depth'.

By this they meant that the church in the global south is growing rapidly – large numbers of people are committing their lives to Christ and joining local Christian communities – but there is a great need for growth to maturity, and the resources which are needed to make that happen. John Stott boiled down this need according to a simple logic.

- God wants his church to grow up in maturity
- The church grows through the word of God
- The word of God comes to churches primarily through preaching

And this led him to ask the basic question: 'What can we do to raise the standards of biblical preaching?'

As a result, he founded several projects which have now come together under the title 'Langham Partnership International'. Supported by believers around the world, LPI seeks to work in fellowship with national leaders in strengthening biblical preaching and teaching in the churches and seminaries in the majority world. It seeks to do so through three programmes.

Langham Preaching partners with national leaders to nurture indigenous preaching movements for pastors and lay preachers all around the world. Such partnership provides on site support for preachers, organising training seminars, providing resources, encouraging preachers' groups and building a local movement committed to Bible exposition.

Langham Literature provides evangelical resources in multiple languages through grants and distribution, and fosters the indigenous creation of resources through sponsored editing and writing and publisher support.

Since church leaders are strongly shaped by those who teach them, the **Langham Scholars** programme provides financial support for evangelical doctoral students from the majority world, so that they may train Christian pastors and leaders – usually at seminary or university level – with sound, biblical teaching. Langham Scholars has supported nearly three hundred scholars from over eighty countries, and has expanded support for doctoral education at key majority world institutions.

Langham Partnership is pleased to work in fellowship with Keswick Ministries in different parts of the world, particularly through its Langham Preaching initiatives. For more information, please contact Jonathan Lamb at: jonathan@langhampartnership.org or 16 Eden Drive, Oxford, OX3 0AB, England.

For more information about the wider work of Langham Partnership, please see our website: www.langhampartnership.org.

KESWICK MINISTRIES

Keswick Ministries is committed to the deepening of the spiritual life in individuals and church communities through the careful exposition and application of Scripture, seeking to encourage the following:

The Lordship of Christ – To encourage submission to the Lordship of Christ in personal and corporate living.

Life Transformation – To encourage a dependency upon the indwelling and fullness of the Holy Spirit for life transformation and effective living.

Evangelism and Mission – To provoke a strong commitment to the breadth of evangelism and mission in the British Isles and worldwide.

Discipleship – To stimulate the discipling and training of people of all ages in godliness, service and sacrificial living.

Unity – To provide a practical demonstration of evangelical unity.

Keswick Ministries is committed to achieving its aims by:

- providing Bible-based training courses for youth workers and young people (via Root 66) and Bible weeks for Christians of all backgrounds who want to develop their skills and learn more.
- promoting the use of books, DVDs and CDs so that Keswick's teaching ministry is brought to a wider audience at home and abroad.
- producing TV and radio programmes so that superb Bible talks can be broadcast to people at home.
- publishing up-to-date details of Keswick's exciting news and events on the website so that people can access material and purchase Keswick products on-line.
- publicising Bible teaching events in the UK and overseas so that Christians of all ages are encouraged to attend 'Keswick' meetings closer to home and grow in their faith.

- putting the residential accommodation of the Convention Centre at the disposal of churches, youth groups, Christian organisations and many others, at very reasonable rates, for holidays and outdoor activities in a stunning location.

If you'd like more details, please look at the website (www.keswickministries.org) or contact the Keswick Ministries office by post, email or telephone, as given below

Keswick Ministries, Convention Centre, Skiddaw Street, Keswick, Cumbria, CA12 4BY

Tel: 017687 80075; Fax 017687 75276; email: info@keswickministries.org

CDs, DVDs, tapes, videos and books

All talks recorded at Keswick, plus many more
audio and video recordings from the Convention,
dating back to 1957, can be ordered from
www.essentialchristian.com
or by calling ICC: 01323 643341

Resource catalogues featuring recent audio and
video recordings of the Keswick Convention can
be obtained from
ICC
Silverdale Road, Eastbourne
BN20 7AB
Tel. 01323 643341; Fax 01323 649240
Some previous annual Keswick volumes (all
published by Authentic Media) can be obtained
from: The Keswick Convention Centre
Skiddaw Street, Keswick, Cumbria, CA12 4BY
Tel. 017687 80075
www.keswickministries.org

or from your local Christian bookseller or direct
from the publishers, Authentic Media, 9 Holdom
Avenue, Bletchley, Milton Keynes, MK1 1QR. Tel.
0800 834315
or from
www.authenticmedia.co.uk